NINJA CREAMi DELUXE COOKBOOK 2024

110+ latest frozen treats recipes to enjoy ice cream, Italian ice, slushi, yogurt, sorbet, gelato, creamiccino, at your fingertips for family-friendly & busy people

Dorene J. Millettes

All right reserved. No part of this publication may be reproduced, distributed, or transmitted in any form or by any means, including photocopying, recording, or other electronic or mechanical methods, without the prior written permission of the publisher, except in the case of brief quotations embodied in critical reviews and certain other noncommercial uses permitted by copyright law. Copyright © Dorene J. Millettes 2024.

TABLE OF CONTENTS

INTRODUCTION
GETTING STARTED WITH YOUR NINJA CREAMI DELUXE
ICE CREAM RECIPES
    STRAWBERRY CHEESECAKE ICE CREAM
    STRAWBERRY ICE CREAM
    COOKIES & CREAM ICE CREAM
    VANILLA ICE CREAM WITH CHOCOLATE CHIPS
    DEATH BY CHOCOLATE ICE CREAM
    ROCKY ROAD & DOUBLE COOKIE ICE CREAM
    SALTED CARAMEL ICE CREAM
    CREAMSICLE ICE CREAM
    PERFECTLY PERSONALIZED ICE CREAM
    BOOZY BERRY SHORTCAKE ICE CREAM
    CHOCOLATE ICE CREAM
    DAIRY-FREE SWEET POTATO & MARSHMALLOW ICE CREAM

GELATO RECIPES
    MAPLE GELATO
    TRIPLE CHOCOLATE GELATO
    VANILLA BEAN GELATO
    RED VELVET GELATO

SLUSHI RECIPES
    PINK LEMONADE SLUSHI
    PINEAPPLE MANGO SLUSHI
    SWEET CREAM SLUSHI
    PINEAPPLE GREEN TEA SLUSHI
    PINEAPPLE ORANGE SLUSHI
    COCONUT MANGO SLUSHI
    ORANGE CREAM SLUSHI
    MANGO SLUSHI

GUAVA SLUSHI
LIME IN THE COCONUT SLUSHI

CREAMICCINO RECIPES
SALTED TRIPLE CHOCOLATE CREAMICCINO
STRAWBERRIES AND CREAMICCINO
VANILLA BEAN CREAMICCINO
PEACHES AND CREAMICCINO
MUDSLIDE
MOCHA CREAMICCINO
FROZEN MATCHA LATTE
DULCE DE LECHE CREAMICCINO
CAFFE SHAKERATO
BROWN SUGAR OAT MILK CREAMICCINO
FROZEN CHAI LATTE

FROZEN YOGURT RECIPES
SUNRISE FROZEN YOGURT
COFFEE PROTEIN ICE CREAM
PINEAPPLE DULCE DE LECHES FROZEN YOGURT
Key Lime Pie Frozen Yogurt
CREAMSICLE FROZEN YOGURT
CHOCOLATE FROZEN YOGURT
STRAWBERRY FROZEN YOGURT

ITALIAN ICE RECIPES
CHERRY LIMEADE ITALIAN ICE
TIGER'S BLOOD ITALIAN ICE
SPIKED BERRY ITALIAN ICE (WITH HOLIDAY TRULY)
WATERMELON ITALIAN ICE
LEMON ITALIAN ICE
BLUEBERRY LEMONADE ITALIAN ICE

SORBET RECIPES
FRESH FRUIT BANANA SORBET
BOOZY PASSION PEACH SORBET
CONCORD GRAPE SORBET

- EASY PINEAPPLE SORBET
- BOOZY STRAWBERRY SORBET

FROZEN DRINK RECIPES
- PALOMA
- MAI TAI
- MANGO MARGARITA
- MANGO LASSI
- FROZEN GRASSHOPPER
- FROZEN GRAPEFRUIT CRUSH
- HURRICANE
- FROZEN PAIN KILLER
- FROZEN LIMONCELLO
- FROZEN KYIV MULE

FINAL THOUGHT AND ENCOURAGEMENT

CONVERSION MEASUREMENT

TROUBLESHOOTING COMMON ISSUES

INTRODUCTION

Hey there, Today, we're diving into the awesome world of making your very own frozen treats at home. Imagine creating ice creams, sorbets, and yogurts that are not just tasty but also made by you – yes, you!

You know how you sometimes buy ice cream from the store? Well, making your own frozen treats is like becoming a dessert wizard. You get to choose the flavors, mix in your favorite stuff, and create something totally unique. It's not just about eating yummy things; it's about having fun while making them.

Meet Your Kitchen Sidekick: Ninja Creami Deluxe

Alright, so we have a super cool kitchen buddy called the Ninja Creami Deluxe. Think of it as your magical tool that helps you turn simple ingredients into fantastic frozen goodies. It's like having a superhero in your kitchen – it can make all sorts of treats, from super creamy ice creams to refreshing sorbets and even frozen yogurts!

Sure, store-bought treats are okay, but making your own is way more exciting. You get to be the boss of your dessert, picking exactly what you want in it. No more limits – you can add fun things like cookies, fruits, or even candies. Homemade treats are like your own tasty experiments!

Making frozen treats isn't just about eating them later. It's about spending time with your family or friends, laughing together, and creating memories. Picture this: everyone gathering in the kitchen, trying out new recipes, and having a blast. These moments make your treats extra special.

The best part? Sharing what you make! Imagine surprising your family with a dessert you created just for them. Or having a party where everyone gets to make their own ice cream creations. It's like giving a yummy gift to your friends and family, and it makes everyone happy!

So, get ready, With your Ninja Creami Deluxe, your kitchen is about to become a magical place where you can create, experiment, and have a ton of fun. Say hello to a world full of tasty adventures, where every scoop brings a smile. Get ready to be the dessert master in your own kitchen!

GETTING STARTED WITH YOUR NINJA CREAMI DELUXE

First things first, let's talk about what the Ninja Creami Deluxe actually does. Picture this – you have a big bowl filled with creamy liquid, maybe some milk, cream, and sugar, along with your favorite flavorings like chocolate, strawberries, or vanilla. Now, imagine that this bowl gets really, really cold, almost like it's been sitting in the freezer for hours.

Once our bowl is nice and frosty, it's time for the Ninja Creami Deluxe to do its thing. You pour your mixture into the bowl, and then the machine starts spinning it around really fast. This is where the magic happens! As the mixture spins, it starts to freeze, turning from liquid to creamy, dreamy frozen goodness.

But wait, there's more! While the mixture is spinning, the Ninja Creami Deluxe also adds a bit of air into the mix. This might sound strange, but it's actually what gives your frozen treats that light and fluffy texture. It's like whipping cream – the more you whip it, the fluffier it gets!

Now, here's the really cool part – you get to customize your creations however you want! Do you want to make chocolate chip cookie dough ice cream? Just add some cookie dough pieces to your mixture before you start churning. Craving something fruity? Throw in some fresh berries or sliced bananas. The possibilities are endless!

As you can see, the Ninja Creami Deluxe isn't just a machine – it's a gateway to a world of frozen delights and culinary adventures. Whether you're making treats for yourself, your family, or your friends, every batch you create is a chance to make memories in the kitchen and share the joy of delicious homemade desserts.

Now, don't worry if your first batch of ice cream doesn't turn out exactly how you imagined. Like any skill, mastering the art of making frozen treats takes practice. The more you experiment, the better you'll get, and soon enough, you'll be churning out creamy creations like a pro!

Essential Tips and Tricks for Success

Tip #1: Freeze Everything

Before you even think about making your frozen treats, make sure to chill out – literally! Pop the bowl and paddle of your Ninja Creami Deluxe into the freezer for at least 24 hours before you plan to use them. This ensures that everything is super cold and ready to work its freezing magic.

Tip #2: Quality Ingredients Matter

Just like with any recipe, the quality of your ingredients can make all the difference. Opt for fresh, high-quality ingredients whenever possible. Whether it's using real vanilla beans instead of extract or sourcing organic fruits for your sorbets, investing in good ingredients will elevate your frozen treats to a whole new level.

Tip #3: Don't Overfill

It can be tempting to fill your Ninja Creami Deluxe to the brim with ingredients, but trust me – less is more! Overfilling can prevent the mixture from churning properly and result in uneven freezing. Stick to the recommended maximum fill line to ensure smooth, creamy results every time.

Tip #4: Get Creative with Flavors

One of the best things about making your own frozen treats is the freedom to get creative with flavors. Don't be afraid to experiment with different combinations – whether it's adding a swirl of caramel to your ice cream or mixing in chunks of your favorite candy bar. The sky's the limit!

Tip #5: Patience is Key

As tempting as it may be to sneak a taste of your frozen treats straight out of the machine, resist the urge! For best results, transfer your finished creation to a freezer-safe container and let it firm up for a couple of hours before serving. Trust me, the wait will be worth it.

Tip #6: Clean Up Right Away

Once you've finished indulging in your delicious desserts, don't forget to clean your Ninja Creami Deluxe right away. This will help prevent any leftover residue from hardening and becoming difficult to remove later on. Plus, it'll ensure that your machine is always ready for your next sweet adventure.

Tip #7: Have Fun and Experiment

Last but not least, don't forget to have fun and let your creativity run wild! The Ninja Creami Deluxe is your ticket to a world of frozen delights, so don't be afraid to try new things and see what works. Whether you're a seasoned pro or a newbie in the kitchen, there's always something new to discover.

Safety Precautions and Maintenance

Safety First: Precautions to Keep in Mind

Read the Manual: Before you dive into making frozen treats, take some time to read the instruction manual that comes with your Ninja Creami Deluxe. It's packed with important information about how to safely operate the machine and avoid any mishaps.

Keep Hands Away: When the machine is in operation, make sure to keep your hands and fingers away from any moving parts, especially the spinning paddle inside the bowl. This will help prevent accidents and ensure a safe churning experience.

Use Caution with Hot Ingredients: If you're making a recipe that requires heating ingredients before freezing, like custards or cooked fruit compotes, use caution when handling hot liquids. Allow them to cool slightly before pouring them into the machine to avoid splashing or burns.

Supervise Children: If you're letting younger siblings or friends help out in the kitchen, make sure to supervise them closely, especially when operating the Ninja Creami Deluxe. It's a fun machine, but it's important to use it safely.

Maintenance Tips

Clean After Each Use: After you've finished making your frozen treats, don't forget to give your Ninja Creami Deluxe a thorough cleaning. Wash the bowl, paddle, and any other removable parts with warm, soapy water, and dry them thoroughly before storing.

Avoid Abrasive Cleaners: When cleaning your Ninja Creami Deluxe, avoid using abrasive cleaners or scouring pads, as they can scratch the surface of the machine. Stick to mild dish soap and a soft sponge to keep your machine looking like new.

Store Properly: When not in use, store your Ninja Creami Deluxe in a cool, dry place away from direct sunlight. This will help prevent any damage to the machine and ensure it's ready for your next frozen treat adventure.

Follow Maintenance Schedule: Finally, be sure to follow any recommended maintenance schedule outlined in the instruction manual. This may include tasks like lubricating moving parts or replacing worn components to keep your machine running smoothly.

Ice cream Recipes

ICE CREAM RECIPES

STRAWBERRY CHEESECAKE ICE CREAM

Prepare for 10 minutes.   Freeze Time: 24 hours.   Serves 6

- 4 ½ tablespoons cream cheese
- ½ cup Domino Golden Sugar
- 1 teaspoon pure vanilla extract
- 1 cup heavy cream / 240g heavy cream
- 2 tablespoons sour cream
- 1 ¼ cups whole milk / 300g whole milk
- Pinch salt
- 2 tablespoons strawberry preserves
- 2 graham crackers, crushed
- 1/3 cup fresh strawberries cut in small cubes

UTENSILS

- Large Bowl

Instruction

1. Microwave cream cheese in a big bowl for 15 seconds. Add the sugar and vanilla, and beat until the mixture resembles frosting, about 2 minutes.
2. Gradually add cream, sour cream, milk, and salt. Mix until smooth and evenly blended.
3. Pour the ingredients into a clean Creami Deluxe Pint until it reaches the Scoopable Max Fill line. Cover and freeze for 24 hours.
4. Take the Deluxe Pint from the freezer and take off the top. Put the Deluxe Pint into the Ninja Creami Deluxe (assembly instructions included).

5. Select ice cream using the dial after pressing FULL. When the ice cream is ready to be served, the machine will stop.
6. Use a spoon to make a 2-inch diameter hole that reaches the bottom of the pint. Add the fresh strawberries, graham crackers, and preserves. Reassemble the pint in the machine and press MIX-IN. When processing is finished, remove from machine and serve.

STRAWBERRY ICE CREAM

Prepare for 15 minutes.   Freeze Time: 24 hours.   Serves 4

- 2 1/4 cups fresh strawberries / 365g fresh strawberries, trimmed, cut in quarters
- 3/4 cup granulated sugar / 150g granulated sugar
- 1 1/2 teaspoons light corn syrup
- 1 1/2 teaspoons lemon juice
- 1 1/2 cups heavy cream

UTENSILS

- Large Bowl
- Fork

Instruction

1. combine strawberries, sugar, corn syrup, and lemon juice In a large mixing bowl. With a fork, crush the strawberries. Allow mixture to settle for 10 minutes, stirring often.
2. Add heavy cream and stir thoroughly.
3. Pour the base into an empty CREAMi Deluxe Pint. Place the storage lid on the pint and for 24 hours freeze it.

4. Remove Deluxe Pint from freezer, then remove lid from Deluxe Pint.
5. For further information on bowl assembly and unit interactions, see the quick start guide.
6. Choose TOP, FULL, or BOTTOM, then pick ICE CREAM.
7. Add mix-ins or serve ice cream from the Deluxe Pint after processing.

COOKIES & CREAM ICE CREAM

Prepare for 5 minutes.   **Total Time: 24hours, 5 minutes.**
Serves 4

- 1 tablespoon + 1 ½ teaspoons cream cheese, softened
- 1/2 cup granulated sugar / 100g granulated sugar
- 1 1/2 teaspoons vanilla extract
- 1 cup + 2 tablespoons heavy cream / 270g heavy cream
- 1 1/2 cups whole milk / 360g whole milk
- 5 chocolate sandwich cookies, broken, for mix-in

UTENSILS

- Microwave-Safe Bowl
- Whisk

Instruction

1. Microwave cream cheese in a large microwave-safe bowl for 10 seconds. Add the sugar and vanilla extract, and stir with a whisk or rubber spatula

until the mixture resembles frosting, which should take approximately 60 seconds.
2. Slowly add heavy cream and milk until sugar is dissolved.
3. Pour the base into an empty CREAMi Deluxe Pint. Place the cover on the Deluxe Pint and for 24 hours freeze it.
4. Remove pint from freezer and then remove lid from pint.
5. Place pint in outer bowl, then install Creamerizer Paddle onto outer bowl lid, and lock the lid assembly on the outer bowl. Then, Place bowl assembly on motor base and twist the handle right to raise the platform and lock in place
6. Choose TOP, FULL, or BOTTOM, then pick ICE CREAM.
7. Use a spoon to form a 1 ½-inch broad grip that reaches the bottom of the pint. Add the broken chocolate sandwich cookies to the hole and process again with the MIX-IN software. After the processing is finished, take the ice cream out of the pint and serve it right away with your preferred toppings.

VANILLA ICE CREAM WITH CHOCOLATE CHIPS

Prepare for 5 minutes. **Total Time: 24hours, 10 minutes.**
Serves 4
- 1 1/2 tablespoons (3/4 ounce) cream cheese / 28g cream cheese
- 1/2 cup granulated sugar / 100g granulated sugar
- 1 1/2 teaspoons vanilla extract
- 1 cup + 2 tablespoons heavy cream
- 1 1/2 cups whole milk
- 1/3 cup mini chocolate chips, for mix-in

UTENSILS
- Rubber Spatula
- Microwave-Safe Bowl

Instruction

1. Microwave cream cheese in a large microwave-safe bowl for 10 seconds. Add the sugar and vanilla extract, and incorporate with a whisk or rubber spatula until the mixture resembles frosting, approximately 60 seconds.
2. Slowly add heavy cream and milk until sugar is dissolved.
3. Pour the base into an empty CREAMi Deluxe Pint. Place the cover on the Deluxe Pint and freeze for 24 hours.
4. Take the Deluxe Pint out of the freezer and remove the lid from deluxe pint. For further information on bowl assembly and unit interactions, see the quick start guide.
5. Choose TOP, FULL, or BOTTOM, then select ICE CREAM.
6. Use a spoon to make a 1 1/2-inch diameter hole in the processed area of the Deluxe Pint. Add chocolate chips to the hole in the Deluxe Pint and repeat the procedure with the same processing mode and MIX-IN software.
7. Remove the ice cream from the Deluxe Pint and serve immediately after processing.

DEATH BY CHOCOLATE ICE CREAM

Prepare for 5 minutes.   **Total Time: 24hours, 5 minutes.**
Serves 4

- 1 tablespoon + 1 ½ teaspoons cream cheese, softened
- 3 tablespoons cocoa powder
- 1/2 cup granulated sugar / 100g granulated sugar
- 1 1/2 teaspoon vanilla extract
- 1 cup + 2 tablespoons heavy cream / 270g heavy cream
- 1 1/2 cups whole milk / 360g whole milk
- 3 tablespoons mini chocolate chips, for mix in
- 3 tablespoons brownie chunks, for mix-in

Instruction

1. In a microwave-safe bowl, combine cream cheese and chocolate powder and microwave for 10 seconds. Mix in the sugar and vanilla extract with a rubber spatula until the consistency resembles frosting, which should take approximately 60 seconds.
2. Slowly add heavy cream and milk until sugar is dissolved.
3. Pour the base into an empty CREAMi Deluxe Pint. Place the lid on the Deluxe Pint and for 24 hours freeze it.
4. Remove deluxe pint from freezer and then remove lid from pint. Place pint in outer bowl, then install Creamerizer Paddle onto outer bowl lid, and lock the lid assembly on the outer bowl. Then, Place bowl assembly on motor base and twist the handle right to raise the platform and lock in place
5. Choose TOP, FULL, or BOTTOM, then pick ICE CREAM.
6. Use a spoon to form a 1 ½-inch broad grip that reaches the bottom of the pint. Add the chocolate chips and brownie pieces to the hole and process again with the MIX-IN software. Remove ice cream from the pint and serve with preferred toppings.

ROCKY ROAD & DOUBLE COOKIE ICE CREAM

Prep Time: 15 minutes.   **Freeze Time: 24 hours.**
Servings: 6

- 1 1/2 tablespoons (3/4 ounce) of cream cheese / 21g cream cheese
- 3 tablespoons cocoa powder
- 1/2 cup granulated sugar / 115g granulated sugar
- 1 1/2 teaspoons vanilla extract
- 1 cup + 2 tablespoons heavy cream / 240ml + 2 tablespoons heavy cream
- 1 1/2 cups whole milk / 360ml whole milk
- 2 quartered chocolate sandwich cookies, for mix-in
- 2 tablespoons cookie dough pieces, for mix-in

BOTTOM HALF - ROCKY ROAD

- 2 tablespoons mini chocolate chips, for mix-in
- 2 tablespoons chopped peanuts, for mix-in
- 2 tablespoons mini marshmallows, for mix-in

UTENSILS

- Large Bowl
- Spoon
- Whisk
- Rubber Spatula

Instructions

1. In a large microwave-safe bowl, add cream cheese and microwave for up to 10 seconds. Add cocoa powder, sugar, and vanilla extract, then whisk until the mixture looks like frosting, about 60 secs.
2. Slowly mix in heavy cream and milk until it is fully combined and sugar is dissolved.
3. Pour the base into an empty CREAMi Deluxe Pint and for 24 hours freeze it.

4. Remove the Deluxe Pint from the freezer and remove the lid. Follow the quick start guide for bowl assembly and unit interaction.
5. Select TOP, then choose ICE CREAM from the dial, create a 1 1/2-inch-wide hole that reaches halfway down the Deluxe Pint with a spoon and then Add chocolate sandwich cookies and cookie dough pieces to the hole and choose TOP and MIX-IN.
6. Scoop out the rocky road ice cream after processing and serve immediately. To process the bottom half of the Deluxe Pint, select BOTTOM, then choose ICE CREAM.
7. Create a 1 1/2-inch-wide hole that reaches the bottom of the Deluxe Pint with a spoon.
8. Add chocolate chips, peanuts, and marshmallows to the hole and select BOTTOM and MIX-IN.
9. After processing, scoop out the ice cream and serve immediately.

SALTED CARAMEL ICE CREAM

Prep: 10 minutes.   **Total Time: 24 hours 10 minutes**
Serving: 4

- 1 1/2 tablespoons softened cream cheese
- 1/2 cup granulated sugar
- 1 1/2 teaspoons caramel extract
- 1 cup + 2 tablespoons heavy cream
- 1 1/2 cups whole milk
- 1 1/2 teaspoons sea salt

Instructions

1. In a medium microwave-safe bowl, microwave the cream cheese for 10 seconds. Add sugar and caramel extract, then whisk or use a rubber spatula until the mixture resembles frosting, about seconds.
2. Gradually add heavy cream and milk, stirring until fully combined and sugar is dissolved.
3. Pour the mixture into an empty CREAMi Deluxe Pint. Cover with the storage lid and for 24 hrs freeze it.
4. Remove the Deluxe Pint from the freezer and the lid from the Deluxe Pint. Add the pour-in into the MAX FILL line. Place the pint in the outer bowl, install the Creamerizer Paddle onto the outer bowl lid, and then lock the lid assembly on the outer bowl.
5. Position the bowl assembly on the motor base and twist the handle right to lift the platform and lock it in place.
6. Choose TOP, FULL, or BOTTOM, then use the dial to select ICE CREAM.
7. Using a spoon, create a 1 ½-inch-wide hole that reaches the bottom of the pint. Add sea salt to the hole and process again using the MIX-IN program.
8. Once processing is complete, remove the ice cream from the pint and serve immediately with desired toppings.

CREAMSICLE ICE CREAM

Prep: 10 minutes.   Total Time: 24 hours 5 minutes
Serving Size: 4
- 1 tablespoon + 1 1/2 teaspoons softened cream cheese
- 1/2 cup granulated sugar / 100g granulated sugar
- 1 1/2 teaspoons orange extract
- 1 cup + 2 tablespoons heavy cream / 270g heavy cream
- 1 1/2 cups whole milk / 360g whole milk

UTENSILS
- Large Bowl
- Whisk
- Rubber Spatula

Instructions

1. In a large microwave-safe bowl, microwave the cream cheese for 10 seconds. Add sugar and orange extract, then combine with a rubber spatula until the mixture resembles frosting for about
2. secs.
3. Slowly mix in heavy cream and milk until it's fully combined and sugar is dissolved.
4. Fill up the mixture into an empty CREAMi Deluxe Pint. Cover with the storage lid and for 24 hours freeze it.
5. Remove the Deluxe Pint from the freezer and the lid from the Deluxe Pint. Add the pour-in into the MAX FILL line.
   Place the pint in the outer bowl, install the Creamerizer Paddle onto the outer bowl lid, and then lock the lid assembly on the outer bowl.
   Position the bowl assembly on the motor base and twist the handle right to lift the platform and lock it in place.
6. Choose TOP, FULL, or BOTTOM, then use the dial to select ICE CREAM.
7. Remove the ice cream from the pint once processing is complete and serve immediately with desired toppings.

PERFECTLY PERSONALIZED ICE CREAM

Prep Time: 5 mins.   **Total Time: 24 hours 5 mins.**   **Servings: 4**

- 1 1/2 tbsp of cream cheese
- 1/2 cup granulated sugar / 100g granulated sugar
- 1 cup + 2 tbsp heavy cream / 270g heavy cream
- 1 1/2 tsp flavor extract of your preference OR 2 tbsp cocoa powder
- 1 1/2 cups whole milk / 360g whole milk
- 1/4 cup + 2 tbsp optional mix-ins of your choice

UTENSILS
- Microwave-Safe Bowl
- Whisk

Instructions

1. Microwave the cream cheese in a large microwave-safe bowl for 10 seconds. Add sugar and flavor extract, then whisk until the mixture resembles frosting.
2. Gradually add heavy cream and milk until the sugar is fully dissolved.
3. Pour the base into an empty CREAMi Deluxe Pint, then cover it with the storage lid and for 24 hrs freeze it.
4. Remove the Deluxe Pint from the freezer and the lid from the Deluxe Pint. Add the pour-in into the MAX FILL line.
5. After freezing, remove the pint from the freezer and take off the lid. Place the pint in the outer bowl and attach the Creamerizer Paddle to the lid, securing the lid assembly.
6. Position the bowl assembly on the motor base, twist the handle to raise the platform and lock it in place.
7. Choose between TOP, FULL, or BOTTOM settings and then use the dial to select ICE CREAM.
8. If you're adding mix-ins, use a spoon to create a 1 ½-inch wide hole reaching the bottom of the pint. It's acceptable for the mixture to exceed the MAX FILL line during this process. Add mix-ins to the hole and then process again using the MIX-IN program.

9. Remove the ice cream from the pint once the processing is complete, and then serve immediately with desired toppings.

BOOZY BERRY SHORTCAKE ICE CREAM

Prep PT5.   Total 24h 10 mins.   Serves 4

- ½ cup strawberries / 83g strawberries, chopped
- ½ cup granulated sugar / 100g granulated sugar, divided
- 1 teaspoon vanilla extract
- 1 cup whole milk / 240g whole milk, or milk substitute
- ¾ cup heavy cream /180g heavy cream, or milk substitute
- 1 ½ ounces vodka / 28g vodka
- 1 ½ ounces cream liqueur / 28g cream liqueur
- Shortbread cookies
- Whipped cream
- Blueberries

UTENSILS

- Medium Bowl

Instructions

1. Add in your chopped strawberries and 3 tablespoons of sugar in a medium bowl, Mash until sugar is mixed with the strawberries. Into the bowl add in another ¼ cup of sugar, vanilla extract, milk and heavy cream. Mix together until combined.
2. Fill the mixture into an empty CREAMi Deluxe Pint. Place the storage lid on the pint and for 24 hours freeze it.
3. After freezing, remove the pint from the freezer and take off the lid. Place the pint in the outer bowl and attach the Creamerizer Paddle to the lid, securing the lid assembly.
4. Position the bowl assembly on the motor base, twist the handle to raise the platform and lock it in place.

5. Select ICE CREAM.
6. Make a 1 ½-inch broad grip with a spoon, reaching the bottom of the pint. Crumble the shortbread cookies to the hole and process again with the MIX-IN software.
7. Re-spin, if needed. When processing is complete, remove ice cream from pint.
8. Serve with strawberries, whipped cream, more shortbread cookies blueberries and Enjoy!

CHOCOLATE ICE CREAM

Prep 15 mins.   Total 24h 15 mins.   Serves 4

- 1 tablespoon + 1 1/2 teaspoons cream cheese, softened
- 3 tablespoons cocoa powder
- 1/2 cup granulated sugar / 100g granulated sugar
- 1 1/2 teaspoon vanilla extract
- 1 cup + 2 tablespoons heavy cream / 270g heavy cream
- 1 1/2 cups whole milk / 360g whole milk

UTENSILS

- Microwave-Safe Bowl
- Whisk

Instructions

1. Add the cream cheese, in a large microwave-safe bowl and microwave for 10 seconds. Combine the cocoa powder, sugar, and vanilla extract with a whisk or rubber spatula until the consistency resembles frosting, which should take about 60 seconds.
2. Slowly add heavy cream and milk until sugar is dissolved.

3. Pour the base into an empty CREAMi Deluxe Pint. Place the storage lid on the pint and for 24 hours freeze it.
4. After freezing, remove the pint from the freezer and take off the lid. Place the pint in the outer bowl and attach the Creamerizer Paddle to the lid, securing the lid assembly.
5. Position the bowl assembly on the motor base, twist the handle to raise the platform and lock it in place.
6. Choose TOP, FULL, or BOTTOM, then choose ICE CREAM using the dial.
7. Once processing is complete, add mix-ins or remove ice cream from pint and then serve immediately.

DAIRY-FREE SWEET POTATO & MARSHMALLOW ICE CREAM

Prep 15 mins.   Freeze Time 24 hours.   Serves 6

- 1 cup sweet potato puree / 262g sweet potato puree
- 1 ripe banana
- ½ cup sugar-free brown sugar / 100g sugar-free brown sugar
- 2 teaspoons vanilla extract
- 2 teaspoons pumpkin pie spice
- 1 cup unsweetened coconut cream / 240g unsweetened coconut cream (only the cream off the top of the can)
- 1 ½ cups unsweetened coconut milk cream / 342g unsweetened coconut milk cream
- 12 large marshmallows

UTENSILS

- Medium Bowl

- Fork
- Whisk
- Sheet Pan
- Aluminum Foil

Instructions

1. Mix the banana and sweet potato puree in a medium-sized bowl using a fork to mash them together evenly. Add the coconut cream, pumpkin pie spice, vanilla extract, brown sugar, and stir well.
2. Fill up the base into an empty CREAMi Deluxe Pint. Place the storage lid on the pint and for 24 hours freeze it.
3. After freezing, remove the pint from the freezer and take off the lid. Place the pint in the outer bowl and attach the Creamerizer Paddle to the lid, securing the lid assembly.
4. Position the bowl assembly on the motor base, twist the handle to raise the platform and lock it in place.
5. Select FULL, then use the dial to choose LITE ICE CREAM.
6. While the ice cream is processing, heat the oven to BROIL and line a baking pan with aluminum foil. Place the marshmallows on the tray and broil for 1 minute (or until the tops brown), then turn and broil for an additional 30 seconds.
7. Keep a close eye on the marshmallows because they can burn very quickly.
8. Once processing is complete, remove ice cream from Deluxe Pint.
9. Top with roasted marshmallows and then serve immediately.

Gelato Recipes

GELATO RECIPES

MAPLE GELATO

Prep Time: 10 mins.   Total Time: 24 hours 25 mins.   Servings: 4

- 6 large egg yolks
- 1 1/2 tbsp maple syrup
- 1/3 cup light brown sugar / 65g light brown sugar
- 1 1/2 tsp maple extract (optional)
- 1/2 cup heavy cream / 120g heavy cream
- 1 1/2 cups whole milk / 192g whole milk

UTENSILS

- Small Saucepan
- Whisk
- Rubber Spatula
- Instant-Read Thermometer
- Fine-Mesh Strainer

Instructions

1. Combine egg yolks, maple syrup, sugar, and maple extract in a small saucepan, whisking until fully combined and sugar is dissolved.
2. Stir in heavy cream and milk until it's well combined.
3. Place the saucepan on the stove over medium heat, stirring constantly until the temp. reaches 165°F–175°F.
4. Remove the base from heat, strain it through a fine mesh strainer into an empty CREAMi Deluxe Pint, and place the pint in an ice bath. Once cooled, cover it with the storage lid and for 24 hrs freeze it.

5. After freezing, remove the Deluxe Pint from the freezer and take off the lid, refer to the quick start guide for bowl assembly and also unit interaction information.
6. Choose between TOP, FULL, or BOTTOM settings and then use the dial to select GELATO.
7. Add mix-ins or remove the gelato from the pint after processing and then serve immediately.

TRIPLE CHOCOLATE GELATO

Prep Time: 15 mins. **Total Time: 24 hours 25 mins.**
Servings: 4

- 6 large egg yolks
- 1/3 cup + 2 tbsp dark brown sugar / 80g dark brown sugar
- 3 tbsp dark cocoa powder
- 1 1/2 tbsp chocolate fudge topping
- 1 1/4 cups heavy cream / 315g heavy cream
- 1 cup whole milk / 240g whole milk
- 3 tbsp chopped chocolate chunks

UTENSILS

- Small Saucepan
- Whisk
- Instant-Read Thermometer
- Fine-Mesh Strainer

Instructions

1. Combine egg yolks, sugar, cocoa powder, and chocolate fudge in a small saucepan, whisking until fully combined and sugar is dissolved.

2. Add heavy cream and milk, stirring until well combined.
3. Heat the mixture on the stove over medium heat, stirring constantly until the temp. reaches 165°F–175°F.
4. Remove from heat, stir in chocolate chunks until melted, strain the base into an empty CREAMi Deluxe Pint, and place it in an ice bath. Once cooled, cover it with the storage lid and for 24 hrs freeze it.
5. After freezing, remove the Deluxe Pint from the freezer and take off the lid, refer to the quick start guide for bowl assembly and also unit interaction information.
6. Choose between TOP, FULL, or BOTTOM settings and then use the dial to select GELATO.
7. Add mix-ins or remove the gelato from the pint after processing and serve immediately.

VANILLA BEAN GELATO

Prep Time: 15 mins.   Total Time: 24 hours 25 mins.   Servings: 4

- 6 large egg yolks
- 1 1/2 tbsp light corn syrup
- 1/3 cup + 1 tbsp granulated sugar / 77g granulated sugar
- 1 1/2 cups heavy cream / 360g heavy cream
- 1 cup whole milk / 240g whole milk
- 1 1/2 whole vanilla beans, split in half lengthwise, scraped

UTENSILS

- Small Saucepan

- Whisk
- Rubber Spatula
- Instant-Read Thermometer
- Fine-Mesh Strainer

Instructions

1. Whisk together egg yolks, corn syrup, and sugar in a small saucepan until fully combined and sugar is dissolved.
2. Add heavy cream, milk, and vanilla bean, stirring until well combined.
3. Heat the mixture on the stove over medium heat, stirring constantly until the temp. reaches 165°F–175°F.
4. Remove from heat, strain the base into an empty CREAMi Deluxe Pint, and place it in an ice bath. Once cooled, cover it with the storage lid and for 24 hrs freeze it.
5. After freezing, remove the Deluxe Pint from the freezer, remove the lid, refer to the quick start guide for bowl assembly and unit interaction information.
6. Choose between TOP, FULL, or BOTTOM settings and then use the dial to select GELATO.
7. Add mix-ins or remove the gelato from the pint after processing and serve immediately.

RED VELVET GELATO

Prep: 15 minutes.   Total Time: 24 hours 15 minutes.   Servings: 2

- 6 large egg yolks
- 1/4 cup + 2 tablespoons granulated sugar / 75g granulated sugar
- 3 tablespoons unsweetened cocoa powder
- 1 1/2 cups whole milk / 360g whole milk
- 1/2 cup heavy whipping cream / 120g heavy (whipping) cream
- 1/4 cup + 2 tablespoons cream cheese / 66g cream cheese, at room temperature

- 1 1/2 teaspoons vanilla extract
- 1 1/2 teaspoons red food coloring

UTENSILS
- Large Bowl
- Small Saucepan
- Whisk
- Instant-Read Thermometer
- Fine-Mesh Strainer
- Rubber Spatula

Instructions

1. Prepare a large bowl with ice water and place it aside.
2. In a small saucepan, whisk together egg yolks, sugar, and cocoa powder until thoroughly combined and the sugar is dissolved. Do not heat.
3. Add milk, heavy cream, cream cheese, vanilla, and food coloring to the mixture, and whisk until well combined.
4. Place the saucepan over medium heat. Cook, stirring constantly with a rubber spatula until the temp. reaches 165°F to 175°F on an instant-read thermometer.
5. Remove the saucepan from the heat and strain the mixture through a fine-mesh strainer into a clean CREAMi Pint. Carefully place the container in the prepared ice water bath to cool, ensuring no water spills into the base.
6. Once the base has cooled, cover the pint with the storage lid and for 24 hours freeze it.
7. Remove the Deluxe Pint from the freezer and the lid from the Deluxe Pint. Add the pour-in into the MAX FILL line. Place the pint in the outer bowl, install the Creamerizer Paddle onto the outer bowl lid, and then lock the lid assembly on the outer bowl. Position the bowl assembly on the motor base and twist the handle right to lift the platform and lock it in place.
8. Choose TOP, FULL, or BOTTOM and then use the dial to select GELATO.
9. Remove the gelato from the pint once the process is completed and then serve immediately.

Slushi Recipes

SLUSHI RECIPES

PINK LEMONADE SLUSHI

Prepare for 3 minutes.   Freeze Time: 24 hours.   Serves 2

- ½ cup pink lemonade powder mix / 113g pink lemonade powder mix
- 1 ¾ cup (14 ounces) hot water / 397g hot water

FOR PROCESSING

- Pour-in: water, alcohol, or juice

Instruction

1. Add pink lemonade powder to an empty CREAMi Deluxe Pint.
2. Fill the pint with hot water up to the drinkable freeze fill level.
3. Stir the mixture until the drink powder is fully dissolved.
4. Cover pint with storage cover and freeze it for 24 hours.
5. Remove pint from freezer and then remove lid from pint. Pour into the DRINKABLE POUR-IN line, After that, Place pint in outer bowl, install Creamerizer Paddle onto outer bowl lid, and lock the lid assembly on the outer bowl. Then, Place bowl assembly on motor base and twist the handle right to raise the platform and lock in place
6. Select FULL, then SLUSHI.
7. Once finished, pour the slushi into a glass and serve immediately.

PINEAPPLE MANGO SLUSHI

Prepare for 5 minutes.   Freeze Time: 24 hours.   Serves 2

- 1 cup fresh pineapple / 180g fresh pineapple, cut into ½-inch pieces
- 1 cup fresh mango / 180g fresh mango, cut into ½-inch pieces
- ⅓ cup granulated sugar / 67g granulated sugar
- ½ to ¾ cup hot water / 118g to 177g hot water

FOR PROCESSING

Pour-in: water, alcohol, or juice

UTENSILS

- Ladle

Instruction

1. Fill an empty CREAMi Deluxe Pint to the DRINKABLE FREEZE FILL line with pineapple and mango slices.
2. Use heavy cooking utensils, such as a ladle or potato smash, to compress the fruit below the DRINKABLE FILL line. Then, add sugar.
3. Fill the pint with hot water to the DRINKABLE FREEZE FILL line.
4. Stir the mixture until the sugar dissolved fully.
5. Cover the pint with a storage cover and freeze for 24 hours.
6. Remove pint from freezer and then remove lid from pint. Pour into the DRINKABLE POUR-IN line, After that Place pint in outer bowl, install Creamerizer Paddle onto outer bowl lid, and lock the lid assembly on the outer bowl. Then, Place bowl assembly on motor base and twist the handle right to raise the platform and lock in place
7. Select FULL, followed by SLUSHI.
8. After processing, pour the slushi into a glass and serve immediately.

SWEET CREAM SLUSHI

Prepare for 3 minutes.   Freeze Time: 24 hours.   Serves 2

FOR FREEZING
- ½ cup sweetened condensed milk / 150g sweetened condensed milk
- 1 ¾ cup water / 420g water

FOR PROCESSING
- Pour-in: water

UTENSILS
- Spoon

Instruction
1. Pour sweetened condensed milk into an empty CREAMi Deluxe Pint.
2. Fill the Deluxe Pint with water up to the DRINKABLE FILL line.
3. Stir to incorporate the ingredients. Place a storage cover on the Deluxe Pint and freeze for 24 hours.
4. Remove Deluxe pint from freezer and then remove lid from deluxe pint. Add pour-in to the MAX FILL line, Place pint in outer bowl, install Creamerizer Paddle onto outer bowl lid, and lock the lid assembly on the outer bowl. Then, Place bowl assembly on motor base and twist the handle right to raise the platform and lock in place
5. Select FULL, then SLUSHI.
6. Transfer frozen slushi to glass and serve immediately.

PINEAPPLE GREEN TEA SLUSHI

Prepare for 3 minutes.   Freeze Time: 24 hours.   Serves 2

FOR FREEZING
- 1 cup + 2 tablespoons green tea
- 1 cup piña colada mix / 230g piña colada mix

FOR PROCESSING
- Pour in: 1/4 cup pineapple juice,
- 1/4 cup green tea, 2 tablespoons lime juice

UTENSILS
- Spoon

Instruction

1. Fill an empty CREAMi Deluxe Pint with green tea and piña colada mix until the DRINKABLE FILL line.
2. Stir to combine the ingredients. Place a storage cover on the Deluxe Pint and freeze for 24 hours.
3. Remove Deluxe pint from freezer and then remove lid from deluxe pint. Add pour-in to the MAX FILL line, Place pint in outer bowl, install Creamerizer Paddle onto outer bowl lid, and lock the lid assembly on the outer bowl. Then, Place bowl assembly on motor base and twist the handle right to raise the platform and lock in place
4. Select FULL, then SLUSHI.
5. Once processed, pour the pineapple green tea slushi into a glass and serve immediately.

PINEAPPLE ORANGE SLUSHI

Prepare for 3 minutes.   Freeze Time: 24 hours.   Serves 2

FOR FREEZING
- 1 cup + 2 tablespoons orange Juice / 280g orange Juice
- 1 cup + 2 tablespoons pineapple Juice / 280g pineapple Juice

FOR PROCESSING
- Pour-in: orange or pineapple Juice

UTENSILS
- Spoon

Instructions
1. Fill an empty CREAMi Deluxe Pint with orange and pineapple juice until the DRINKABLE FILL line.
2. Stir to combine the ingredients. Place a storage cover on the Deluxe Pint and freeze for 24 hours.
3. Remove Deluxe pint from freezer and then remove lid from deluxe pint. Add pour-in to the MAX FILL line, Place pint in outer bowl, install Creamerizer Paddle onto outer bowl lid, and lock the lid assembly on the outer bowl. Then, Place bowl assembly on motor base and twist the handle right to raise the platform and lock in place
4. Select FULL, then SLUSHI.
5. Transfer frozen slushi to a glass and serve immediately.

COCONUT MANGO SLUSHI

Prep: 5 minutes.   Freeze Time: 24 hours.   Serves: 2

Ingredients for Freezing:
- 1 1/2 cups of mango nectar / 398g mango nectar
- 2/3 cup of coconut milk / 167g coconut milk

For processing:
- Pour-in: Mango nectar

UTENSILS
- Spoon

Instructions

1. Pour the mango nectar and coconut milk in an empty CREAMi Deluxe Pint up to the DRINKABLE FILL line.
2. Stir the mixture until well combined. Place the storage lid on the Deluxe Pint and for 24 hrs freeze it.
3. Select FULL, then use the dial to choose SLUSHI.
4. Transfer the slushi to a glass after processing is complete and then serve immediately.

ORANGE CREAM SLUSHI

Preparation Time: 5 minutes.   Freeze Time: 24 hours.   Serves: 2

For Freezing:
- 1/2 cup orange drink mix / 115g orange drink mix
- 1 3/4 cup warm water / 403g warm water

For Processing
- Pour-in: half and half

UTENSILS
- Spoon

Instructions

1. Place the orange drink mix into an empty CREAMi Deluxe Pint.
2. Pour the warm water in the Deluxe Pint up to the DRINKABLE FILL line.
3. Stir to dissolve the drink mix completely. Place the storage lid on the Deluxe Pint and then freeze for 24 hrs.
4. Remove the Deluxe Pint from the freezer and the lid from the Deluxe Pint. Add the pour-in into the MAX FILL line. Place the pint in the outer bowl, install the Creamerizer Paddle onto the outer bowl lid, and then lock the lid assembly on the outer bowl.
5. Position the bowl assembly on the motor base and twist the handle right to lift the platform and lock it in place.
6. Select FULL, then use the dial to choose SLUSHI.
7. When processing is complete, transfer the Orange Cream Slush to a glass then serve immediately.

MANGO SLUSHI

Preparation: 2 minutes.   Freeze Time: 24 hours.   Serves: 2

For Freezing:

- 1 cup (approx. 5 ounces) frozen mango chunks / 142g frozen mango chunks
- 1 1/2 cups mango nectar / 377g mango nectar

For Processing:

- - Pour-in: mango nectar

UTENSILS

- Spoon

Instructions

1. Place the mango chunks into an empty CREAMi Deluxe Pint.
2. Pour the mango nectar in the Deluxe Pint up to the DRINKABLE FILL line.
3. Stir to combine the mixture. Then place the storage lid on the Deluxe Pint and for 24 hours freeze it.
4. Remove the Deluxe Pint from the freezer and the lid from the Deluxe Pint. Add the pour-in into the MAX FILL line. Place the pint in the outer bowl, install the Creamerizer Paddle onto the outer bowl lid, and then lock the lid assembly on the outer bowl.
5. Position the bowl assembly on the motor base and twist the handle right to lift the platform and lock it in place.
6. Select FULL, then after use the dial to choose SLUSHI.
7. When processing is complete, transfer the slushi to a glass and then serve immediately.

GUAVA SLUSHI

Preparation: 8 minutes.   Freeze Time: 24 hours.   Servings: 2

Ingredients for Freezing:
- 1 3/4 cups guava nectar / 420g guava nectar
- 1/4 cup orange juice / 60g orange juice
- 2 tablespoons lime juice
- 1/4 pineapple, cut into 1-inch pieces
- 2 tablespoons simple syrup

Ingredients for Processing:
- - Equal parts triple sec and dark rum

UTENSILS
- Spoon

Instructions

1. Pour all the juices, pineapple chunks, and simple syrup in an empty CREAMi Deluxe Pint up to the DRINKABLE FILL line.
2. Stir the mixture to combine. Place the storage lid on the Deluxe Pint and for 24 hrs freeze it.
3. Remove the Deluxe Pint from the freezer and the lid from the Deluxe Pint. Add the pour-in into the MAX FILL line. Place the pint in the outer bowl, install the Creamerizer Paddle onto the outer bowl lid, and then lock the lid assembly on the outer bowl.
4. Position the bowl assembly on the motor base and twist the handle right to lift the platform and lock it in place.
5. Select FULL, then use the dial to choose SLUSHI.
6. Transfer the guava slush to a glass once processed and then serve immediately.

LIME IN THE COCONUT SLUSHI

Prep 5 mins.   Freeze Time 24 hours.   Serves 2

Ingredients for Freezing:
- 1/2 cup granulated sugar / 100g granulated sugar
- 1 cup warm water / 236g warm water
- 1/3 cup lime juice / 77g lime juice
- 3/4 cup coconut milk / 188g coconut milk

Ingredients for Processing (Pour-in):
- - Water

UTENSILS
- Spoon

Instructions

1. Place the sugar in an empty CREAMi Deluxe Pint and warm then stir until the sugar is totally dissolved.
2. Add lime juice and coconut milk to the pint up to the DRINKABLE FILL line.
3. Stir well and freeze with the storage lid for 24 hours.
4. Remove the Deluxe Pint from the freezer and the lid from the Deluxe Pint. Add the pour-in into the MAX FILL line. Place the pint in the outer bowl, install the Creamerizer Paddle onto the outer bowl lid, and then lock the lid assembly on the outer bowl.
5. Position the bowl assembly on the motor base and twist the handle right to lift the platform and lock it in place.
6. Select FULL, then choose the SLUSHI setting.
7. Once processed, transfer the Slushi to a glass and then serve right away.

CREAMICCINO RECIPES

SALTED TRIPLE CHOCOLATE CREAMICCINO

Prepare for 3 minutes.   Freeze Time: 24 hours.   Serves 3

FOR FREEZING
- 1/2 cup hot chocolate powdered mix / 113g hot chocolate powdered mix
- Big pinch of salt
- 2 cups warm chocolate milk / 490g warm chocolate milk

FOR PROCESSING
- Pour-in: equal parts crème de cacao and chocolate milk

UTENSILS
- Spoon

Instruction

1. Add hot chocolate mix and salt to an empty CREAMi Deluxe Pint.
2. Fill the Deluxe Pint with warm chocolate milk until the DRINKABLE FILL line.
3. Stir the mixture. Place the cover on the Deluxe Pint and freeze for 24 hours.
4. Remove Deluxe pint from freezer and then remove lid from deluxe pint. Add pour-in to the MAX FILL line, Place pint in outer bowl, install Creamerizer Paddle onto outer bowl lid, and lock the lid assembly on the outer bowl. Then, Place bowl assembly on motor base and twist the handle right to raise the platform and lock in place
5. Select FULL, followed by CREAMICCINO on the dial.

6. Transfer the frozen salted triple chocolate to a glass and then serve immediately. Garnish with more sea salt.

STRAWBERRIES AND CREAMICCINO

Prepare for 3 minutes.   Freeze Time: 24 hours.   Serves 2

FOR FREEZING
- 1 cup diced strawberries / 200g diced strawberries
- 1 cup water / 230g water
- 2/3 cup sweetened condensed milk / 200g sweetened condensed milk

FOR PROCESSING
- Pour-in: water

UTENSILS
- Spoon

Instructions

1. Fill an empty CREAMi Deluxe Pint with strawberries, water, and sweetened condensed milk to the DRINKABLE FILL line.
2. Stir to combine mixture. Place the cover on the Deluxe Pint and freeze for 24 hours.
3. Remove Deluxe pint from freezer and then remove lid from deluxe pint. Add pour-in to the MAX FILL line, Place pint in outer bowl, install Creamerizer Paddle onto outer bowl lid, and lock the lid assembly on the outer bowl. Then, Place bowl assembly on motor base and twist the handle right to raise the platform and lock in place
4. Select FULL, followed by CREAMICCINO on the dial.
5. Transfer the frozen drink to a glass and serve right away.

VANILLA BEAN CREAMICCINO

Prepare for 3 minutes.   Freeze Time: 24 hours.   Serves 3

FOR FREEZING
- 2/3 cup sweetened condensed milk / 200g sweetened condensed milk
- 1 ½ cup + 2 tablespoons water / 390g water
- 1 teaspoon vanilla bean paste

FOR PROCESSING
- Pour-in: Water

Instructions

1. Fill an empty CREAMi Deluxe Pint with sweetened condensed milk, water, and vanilla bean paste to the DRINKABLE FILL line.
2. Stir to blend mixture. Place the cover on the Deluxe Pint and freeze for 24 hours.
3. Remove Deluxe pint from freezer and then remove lid from deluxe pint. Add pour-in to the MAX FILL line, Place pint in outer bowl, then install Creamerizer Paddle onto outer bowl lid, and lock the lid assembly on the outer bowl. Then, Place bowl assembly on motor base and twist the handle right to raise the platform and lock in place
4. Select FULL, followed by CREAMICCINO on the dial.
5. Transfer the frozen drink to a glass and serve right away.

PEACHES AND CREAMICCINO

Preparation: 3 minutes.   Freeze Time: 24 hours.   Serves: 2

Freezing Ingredients:
- 2/3 cup sweetened condensed milk / 204g sweetened condensed milk
- 1 cup water / 230g water
- 2 ripe peaches, diced

For Processing:
- -Pour-in: water

UTENSILS

- Spoon

Instructions

1. Pour the sweetened condensed milk, water, and peaches in an empty CREAMi Deluxe Pint up to the DRINKABLE FILL line.
2. Stir to combine the mixture. Then, place the storage lid on the Deluxe Pint and for 24 hours freeze it.
3. Remove the Deluxe Pint from the freezer, and then remove the lid. Add pour-in to the MAX FILL line. Place the pint in the outer bowl, install the Creamerizer Paddle onto the outer bowl lid, and then lock the lid assembly on the outer bowl.
4. Position the bowl assembly on the motor base and then twist the handle right to raise the platform and lock it in place.
5. Select FULL and then use the dial to select CREAMICCINO.
6. Transfer the frozen drink to a glass when processing is complete and serve immediately.

MUDSLIDE

Preparation Time: 8 minutes.   Freeze Time: 24 hours.   Serves: 2

For Freezing:
- 1 3/4 cups half & half / 403g half & half
- 1/4 cup hot espresso / 58g hot espresso
- 1/4 cup chocolate sauce / 78g chocolate sauce

For Processing (Pour-in):
- - Equal parts vodka, coffee liqueur, and Irish cream

UTENSILS
- Spoon

Instructions

1. Pour the half and half, Chocolate sauce, and Expresso into the Deluxe Pint up to the DRINKABLE FILL line.
2. Stir to combine the mixture. Place the storage lid on the Deluxe Pint and for 24 hrs freeze it.
3. Remove the Deluxe Pint from the freezer and the lid from the Deluxe Pint. Add the pour-in into the MAX FILL line. Place the pint in the outer bowl, install the Creamerizer Paddle onto the outer bowl lid, and then lock the lid assembly on the outer bowl.
4. Position the bowl assembly on the motor base and twist the handle right to lift the platform and lock it in place.
5. Select FULL and then use the dial to choose CREAMICCINO.
6. Transfer the frozen Mudslide to a glass when processing is complete and serve right away.

MOCHA CREAMICCINO

Prep Time: 5 minutes.   Freeze Time: 24 hours.   Serves: 2

For Freezing:
- 1/2 cup powdered hot chocolate / 115g powdered hot chocolate
- 4 shots hot espresso (approximately ½ cup)
- 1 1/2 cups whole milk / 360g whole milk

For Processing
- Pour-in: Whole milk

UTENSILS
- Spoon

Instructions

1. Firstly, Place the hot chocolate mix in an empty CREAMi Deluxe Pint.
2. Pour the hot espresso into the Deluxe Pint and stir thoroughly until the chocolate mix is dissolved.
3. Add the milk into the Deluxe Pint up to the DRINKABLE FILL line.
4. Stir to combine the mixture. Place the storage lid on the Deluxe Pint and for 24 hrs freeze it.
5. Remove the Deluxe Pint from the freezer and the lid from the Deluxe Pint. Add the pour-in into the MAX FILL line. Place the pint in the outer bowl, install the Creamerizer Paddle onto the outer bowl lid, and then lock the lid assembly on the outer bowl.
6. Position the bowl assembly on the motor base and twist the handle right to lift the platform and lock it in place.
7. Select FULL and then use the dial to choose CREAMICCINO.
8. When processing is complete, transfer the frozen drink to a glass and then serve immediately.

FROZEN MATCHA LATTE

Prep: 5 minutes. Freeze Time: 24 hours.   Serves: 2

For Freezing:
- 1/2 cup granulated sugar / 100g granulated sugar
- 1 3/4 cups warm water / 420g warm water
- 2 teaspoons matcha powder

For Processing:
- - Pour-in: milk of choice

UTENSILS
- Spoon

Instructions

1. Place the sugar and matcha powder in an empty CREAMi Deluxe Pint. Pour the warm water to the Deluxe Pint up to the DRINKABLE FILL line.
2. Stir to combine the mixture until the sugar is dissolved. Place the storage lid on the Deluxe Pint and for 24 hrs freeze it.
3. Remove the Deluxe Pint from the freezer and the lid from the Deluxe Pint. Add the pour-in into the MAX FILL line. Place the pint in the outer bowl, install the Creamerizer Paddle onto the outer bowl lid, and then lock the lid assembly on the outer bowl.
4. Position the bowl assembly on the motor base and twist the handle right to lift the platform and lock it in place.
5. Select FULL and then after use the dial to select CREAMICCINO.
6. Transfer the frozen matcha latte to a glass when processing is complete and serve immediately.

DULCE DE LECHE CREAMICCINO

Prep: 3 mins.   Freeze Time: 24 hours.   Serves: 2

Ingredients for Freezing:
- 2/3 cup canned Dulce de Leche / 203g canned Dulce de Leche
- 1 1/2 cups + 2 tablespoons water / 390g water

Ingredients for Processing (Pour-in):
- - Water

UTENSILS
- Spoon

Instructions

1. Pour the Dulce de Leche and water up to the DRINKABLE FILL line into an empty CREAMi Deluxe Pint.
2. Stir the mixture until combined. Place the storage lid on the Deluxe Pint and for 24 hrs freeze it.
3. Remove the Deluxe Pint from the freezer and the lid from the Deluxe Pint. Add the pour-in into the MAX FILL line. Place the pint in the outer bowl, install the Creamerizer Paddle onto the outer bowl lid, and then lock the lid assembly on the outer bowl.
4. Position the bowl assembly on the motor base and twist the handle right to lift the platform and lock it in place.
5. Select FULL and then use the dial to choose CREAMICINNO.
6. Transfer the frozen drink to a glass once the process is complete and serve immediately.

CAFFE SHAKERATO

Total Time: 24 hours and 3 minutes.   Serves: 2

Ingredients for Freezing:
- 1/2 cup of granulated sugar / 100g granulated sugar
- 1 3/4 cups of warm strong coffee / 420g warm strong coffee

Ingredients For Processing:
- Pour-in: 1/3 cup of amaretto
- 1/3 cup of cold brew

UTENSILS
- Spoon

Instructions

1. Place the sugar into an empty CREAMi Deluxe Pint. Pour the warm coffee up unto the DRINKABLE FILL line and stir until the sugar is completely dissolved.
2. Place the storage lid on the Deluxe Pint and for 24 hrs freeze it.
3. Remove the Deluxe Pint from the freezer and the lid from the Deluxe Pint. Add the pour-in into the MAX FILL line. Place the pint in the outer bowl, install the Creamerizer Paddle onto the outer bowl lid, and then lock the lid assembly on the outer bowl.
4. Position the bowl assembly on the motor base and twist the handle right to lift the platform and lock it in place.
5. Select FULL and then use the dial to choose CREAMICCINO.
6. Transfer the frozen Caffe to a glass after processing is complete, and serve immediately. It pairs wonderfully with biscotti.

BROWN SUGAR OAT MILK CREAMICCINO

Prep: 5 minutes.   Freeze Time: 24 hours.   Serves: 2

FOR FREEZING
- 1/2 cup packed brown sugar / 100g brown sugar, packed
- 4 shots of hot espresso (approximately 1/2 cup)
- 1 1/4 cups oat milk / 260g oat milk

FOR PROCESSING
- - Pour-in: oat milk

UTENSILS
- Spoon

Instructions

1. Place the brown sugar in an empty CREAMi Deluxe Pint. Pour the hot espresso over the sugar and then stir until the sugar is dissolved. Add oat milk up to the DRINKABLE FILL line and stir until combined.
2. Place the storage lid on the Deluxe Pint and for 24 hrs freeze it.
3. Remove the Deluxe Pint from the freezer and the lid from the Deluxe Pint. Add the pour-in into the MAX FILL line. Place the pint in the outer bowl, install the Creamerizer Paddle onto the outer bowl lid, and then lock the lid assembly on the outer bowl.
4. Position the bowl assembly on the motor base and twist the handle right to lift the platform and lock it in place.
5. Select FULL and then use the dial to select CREAMICINNO.
6. Transfer the frozen drink to a glass after processing is complete, and then serve immediately.

FROZEN CHAI LATTE

Prep Time: 3 minutes.   Freeze Time: 24 hours.   Servings: 2

- 1 cup + 2 tablespoons (9 ounces) Chai tea concentrate / 255ml Chai tea concentrate
- 1 cup + 2 tablespoons (9 ounces) whole milk / 255ml whole milk

For Processing:
- Pour-in: chai tea concentrate

UTENSILS
- Spoon

Instructions

1. Pour the Chai tea concentrate in an empty CREAMi Deluxe Pint.
2. Pour the milk in the Deluxe Pint up to the DRINKABLE FILL line.
3. Stir the mixture until well combined and then Place the storage lid on the Deluxe Pint and for 24 hrs freeze it.
4. Remove the Deluxe Pint from the freezer and then remove the lid.
5. Add the pour-in up to the MAX FILL line.
6. Follow the quick start guide for bowl assembly and unit interaction.
7. Select FULL and then choose CREAMICCINO from the dial.
8. Transfer the frozen chai latte to a glass once processed
9. Serve immediately.

Frozen Yogurt Recipes

FROZEN YOGURT RECIPES

SUNRISE FROZEN YOGURT

Prepare for 5 minutes.   Freeze Time: 24 hours.   Serves 6

- 1 1/2 cups nonfat vanilla Greek yogurt / 430g nonfat vanilla Greek yogurt
- 1/4 cup maple syrup / 60g maple syrup
- 1 cup canned coconut cream / 240g canned coconut cream
- 1 1/2 cups mango chunks / 250g mango chunks, cut into 1-inch pieces

UTENSILS

- Medium Bowl
- Whisk
- Rubber Spatula

Instructions

1. Mix yogurt, maple syrup, and coconut cream in a medium bowl until well blended. Next, fold in the mango chunks using a rubber spatula.
2. Pour the yogurt mixture into an empty CREAMi Deluxe Pint. Place the storage cover on the pint and freeze for 24 hours.
3. Remove pint from freezer and then remove lid from pint. Place the pint in the outer bowl, install the Creamerizer Paddle onto the outer bowl lid, and then lock the lid assembly on the outer bowl.
4. Then, Place bowl assembly on motor base and twist the handle right to raise the platform and lock in place
5. Choose FULL as the processing zone and FROZEN YOGURT.
6. Transfer froyo to a dish and serve soon after processing.

COFFEE PROTEIN ICE CREAM

Prepare for 3 minutes.   Freeze Time: 24 hours.   Serves 6

- 3 cups Chocolate Fairlife CorePower Protein Shake / 710g Chocolate Fairlife CorePower Protein Shake
- 1 tablespoon chocolate pudding mix
- 3 tablespoons cocoa powder
- 3 tablespoons instant espresso

UTENSILS

- Whisk

Instructions

1. Pour the chocolate protein shake, pudding mix, cocoa powder, and espresso powder into a clean CREAMi Deluxe Pint. Whisk to blend. Place a cover on the pint and freeze for 24 hours. Remove pint from freezer and then remove lid from pint. Place the pint in the outer bowl, install the Creamerizer Paddle onto the outer bowl lid, and then lock the lid assembly on the outer bowl. Then, Place bowl assembly on motor base and twist the handle right to raise the platform and lock in place
2. Choose FROZEN YOGURT. Re-spin as needed.
3. Remove ice cream from pint once processed. Top with your desired toppings and then serve immediately.

PINEAPPLE DULCE DE LECHES FROZEN YOGURT

Preparation: 5 minutes.   Freeze Time: 24 hours.   Serves: 6

Freezing Ingredients:
- 2 cups whole milk vanilla yogurt / 490g whole milk vanilla yogurt
- 3 tablespoons canned dulce de leche
- 1 cup of pineapple chunks / 225g pineapple chunks, cut into 1-inch pieces

UTENSILS
- Whisk
- Medium Bowl
- Rubber Spatula
- Measuring Cups

Instructions

1. In a medium bowl, whisk together the yogurt and dulce de leche until it is evenly combined. With a rubber spatula to fold in the pineapple chunks.
2. Pour the yogurt mixture in an empty CREAMi Deluxe Pint. Place the storage lid on the pint and for 24 hrs freeze it.
3. Remove the Deluxe Pint from the freezer, and then remove the lid. Place the pint in the outer bowl, install the Creamerizer Paddle onto the outer bowl lid, and then lock the lid assembly on the outer bowl.
4. Position the bowl assembly on the motor base and twist the handle right to lift the platform and lock it in place.
5. Select FULL, and use the dial to select FROZEN YOGURT.
6. When processing is complete, transfer the froyo to a bowl and serve right away.

KEY LIME PIE FROZEN YOGURT

Prep 2 mins.   Freeze Time 24 hours.   Serves 6

Ingredients for Freezing:
- 3 cups of whole milk key lime pie flavored yogurt / 680g whole milk key lime pie flavored yogurt

Ingredients for Processing:
- 3 graham cracker squares, broken into bite-sized pieces

UTENSILS
- Spoon

Instructions

1. Pour yogurt into an empty CREAMi Deluxe Pint up to the MAX FILL line.
2. Place the storage lid on the Deluxe Pint and for 24 hrs freeze it.
3. Remove the Deluxe Pint from the freezer and the lid from the Deluxe Pint. Add the pour-in into the MAX FILL line. Place the pint in the outer bowl, install the Creamerizer Paddle onto the outer bowl lid, and then lock the lid assembly on the outer bowl.
4. Position the bowl assembly on the motor base and twist the handle right to lift the platform and lock it in place.
5. Select FULL, TOP, or BOTTOM and use the dial to select FROZEN YOGURT.
6. Create 1 1/2-inch wide hole that reaches the bottom of the Deluxe Pint using a spoon and then add graham cracker pieces through a hole in the yogurt using the MIX-IN program.
7. Transfer the frozen yogurt to a bowl once processed and then serve immediately.

CREAMSICLE FROZEN YOGURT

Prep: 5 minutes.   Freeze Time: 24 hours.   Serves: 6

- 2 1/4 cups of whole milk vanilla yogurt / 551g whole milk vanilla yogurt
- 1/4 cup plus 2 tablespoons of orange marmalade
- 1/4 cup plus 2 tablespoons of orange juice
- 1 vanilla bean, split into half lengthwise, and scraped

UTENSILS

- Medium Bowl
- Whisk

Instructions

1. In a medium bowl, thoroughly whisk together all the ingredients until evenly combined.
2. Pour the yogurt mixture into an empty CREAMi Deluxe Pint. Secure the storage lid on the pint and for 24 hrs freeze it.
3. Remove the Deluxe Pint from the freezer and the lid from the Deluxe Pint. Add the pour-in into the MAX FILL line. Place the pint in the outer bowl, install the Creamerizer Paddle onto the outer bowl lid, and then lock the lid assembly on the outer bowl.
4. Position the bowl assembly on the motor base and twist the handle right to lift the platform and lock it in place.
5. Choose the processing zone FULL, then select FROZEN YOGURT.
6. Transfer the frozen yogurt to a bowl once process is complete and then serve immediately.

CHOCOLATE FROZEN YOGURT

Prep: 5 minutes.   Freeze Time: 24 hours.   Serves: 6

- 2 1/4 cups of whole milk vanilla yogurt / 551g whole milk vanilla yogurt
- 3/4 cup of chocolate hazelnut spread / 188g chocolate hazelnut spread
- 3 tablespoons of cocoa powder

UTENSILS

- Medium Bowl
- Whisk

Instructions

1. In a medium bowl, whisk together all of the ingredients until thoroughly combined.
2. Pour the yogurt mixture into an empty CREAMi Deluxe Pint. Place the storage lid on the Deluxe Pint and for 24 hrs freeze it.
3. Remove the Deluxe Pint from the freezer and the lid from the Deluxe Pint. Add the pour-in into the MAX FILL line. Place the pint in the outer bowl, install the Creamerizer Paddle onto the outer bowl lid, and then lock the lid assembly on the outer bowl.
4. Position the bowl assembly on the motor base and twist the handle right to lift the platform and lock it in place.
5. Choose the processing zone FULL and then select FROZEN YOGURT.
6. Transfer the frozen yogurt to a bowl once the process is completed and then serve immediately.

STRAWBERRY FROZEN YOGURT

Prep: 2 minutes.   Freeze Time: 24 hours.   Serves: 6

- 3 cups (24 ounces) of whole milk strawberry yogurt / 680g whole milk strawberry yogurt

Instructions

1. Pour the yogurt in an empty CREAMi Deluxe Pint up to the MAX FILL line. Place the storage lid on the Deluxe Pint and for 24 hrs freeze it.
2. Remove the Deluxe Pint from the freezer and then remove the lid. Refer to the quick start guide for bowl assembly and also unit interaction information.
3. Select TOP, FULL, or BOTTOM, then use the dial to choose FROZEN YOGURT.
4. Transfer the frozen yogurt to a bowl when processing is complete, and serve immediately.

Italian Ice Recipes

ITALIAN ICE RECIPES

CHERRY LIMEADE ITALIAN ICE

Prepare for 3 minutes. Freeze Time: 24 hours. Serves 6

- 2 cups (16 ounces) room-temperature lemonade / 454g lemonade
- ½ cup (4 ounces) Lime syrup / 113g Lime syrup
- ½ cup (4 ounces) Cherry syrup / 113g Cherry syrup

Instructions

1. Fill the CREAMi Deluxe Pint with lemonade and syrup to the SCOOPABLE MAX FILL line.
2. Stir mixture until syrup is fully dissolved. Place the pint in the freezer for 24 hours with the storage cover on.
3. Remove pint from freezer and then remove lid from pint. Place the pint in outer bowl, then install Creamerizer Paddle onto outer bowl lid, and lock the lid assembly on the outer bowl. Then, Place bowl assembly on motor base and twist the handle right to raise the platform and lock in place
4. Choose TOP, FULL, or BOTTOM, then select ITALIAN ICE.
5. Transfer the processed Italian ice to a bowl and serve immediately.

TIGER'S BLOOD ITALIAN ICE

Prepare for 3 minutes.   Freeze Time: 24 hours.   Serves 6

- ¾ cup (6 ounces) Tiger's Blood syrup / 170g Tiger's Blood syrup
- 2 ¼ (18 ounces) hot water / 510g hot water

Instruction

1. Pour syrup into an empty CREAMi Deluxe Pint.
2. Fill the pint with hot water till the SCOOPABLE MAX FILL line.
3. Stir the mixture until the syrup is fully dissolved. Place the storage cover on the pint and freeze for 24 hours.
4. Remove pint from freezer and then remove lid from pint. Place the pint in outer bowl, then install Creamerizer Paddle onto outer bowl lid, and lock the lid assembly on the outer bowl. Then, Place bowl assembly on motor base and twist the handle right to raise the platform and lock in place
5. Choose TOP, FULL, or BOTTOM, then select ITALIAN ICE.
6. Transfer processed Italian ice to a bowl and serve immediately.

SPIKED BERRY ITALIAN ICE (WITH HOLIDAY TRULY)

Prepare for 2 minutes.   Total Time: 24hours, 2 minutes.   Serves 2

- 1 can TRULY Berry Bramble Seltzer
- 1 teaspoon blueberry or grape jelly
- 1 teaspoon half & half
- Whipped cream, for garnish
- Blueberries, for garnish

- Fresh mint, for garnish

UTENSILS
- Spoon
- Whisk
- Large Bowl

Instructions

1. Combine seltzer, jelly, and half & half in a large bowl. Whisk well. Then, pour the base into an empty CREAMi Pint. Place the storage cover on the Deluxe Pint and for 24 hours freeze it.
2. Remove pint from freezer and then remove lid from pint. Place the pint in outer bowl, then install Creamerizer Paddle onto outer bowl lid, and lock the lid assembly on the outer bowl. Then, Place bowl assembly on motor base and twist the handle right to raise the platform and lock in place
3. Choose FULL as the processing zone and then ITALIAN ICE.
4. Pour the Italian ice into a glass and garnish with whipped cream, blueberries, and fresh mint.

WATERMELON ITALIAN ICE

Prep Time: 3 minutes.   Freeze Time: 24 hours.   Servings: 6

- 3/4 cup (6 ounces) watermelon syrup / 170ml watermelon syrup
- 2 1/4 cups (18 ounces) hot water / 510ml hot water

UTENSILS
- Spoon

Instructions

1. Pour the watermelon syrup into an empty CREAMi Deluxe Pint.
2. Pour the hot water into the Deluxe Pint up unto the MAX FILL line.
3. Stir the mixture until the syrup is completely dissolved and Place the storage lid on the Deluxe Pint and for 24 hrs freeze it.
4. Remove the Deluxe Pint from the freezer and remove the lid. Refer to the quick start guide for bowl assembly and also unit interaction information.
5. Choose the setting (TOP, FULL, or BOTTOM) and select ITALIAN ICE using the dial.
6. Transfer the Italian ice to a bowl after processing is complete and serve immediately.

LEMON ITALIAN ICE

Prep: 3 minutes.   Freeze Time: 24 hours.   Serves: 6

- 1/2 cup lemonade powdered drink mix / 113g lemonade powdered drink mix
- 2 1/2 cups (20 ounces) hot water / 591ml hot water

UTENSILS

- Spoon

Instructions

1. Pour the drink powder in an empty CREAMi Deluxe Pint.
2. Pour hot water in the Deluxe Pint up to the MAX FILL line.
3. Stir to combine the mixture until the drink powder is fully dissolved.
4. Place the storage lid on the Deluxe Pint and for 24 hrs freeze it.

5. Remove the Deluxe Pint from the freezer and then remove the lid. Refer to quick start guide for the bowl assembly and unit interaction information.
6. Select (TOP, FULL, or BOTTOM) then use the dial to choose ITALIAN ICE
7. Transfer the Italian ice to a serving bowl after processing is complete, and then serve immediately.

BLUEBERRY LEMONADE ITALIAN ICE

Prep Time: 5 minutes.   Freeze Time: 24 hours.   Servings: 6

- 3 tablespoons blueberry jelly
- 2 ½ cups (20 ounces) lemonade

UTENSILS

- Measuring Cups

Instructions

1. Add the blueberry jelly and 1/2 cup of lemonade in an empty CREAMi Deluxe Pint.
2. Stir the mixture until the jelly is dissolved into the lemonade, add the remaining lemonade up to the MAX FILL LINE and whisk until combined.
3. Place the storage lid on the Deluxe Pint and then for 24 hrs freeze it.
4. Remove the Deluxe Pint from the freezer and the lid from the Deluxe Pint. Add the pour-in into the MAX FILL line. Place the pint in the outer bowl, install the Creamerizer Paddle onto the outer bowl lid, and then lock the lid assembly on the outer bowl. Position the bowl assembly on the motor base and twist the handle right to lift the platform and lock it in place.
5. Select TOP, FULL, or BOTTOM, and use the dial to select ITALIAN ICE.
6. Transfer the Italian Ice to a serving bowl after processing and serve immediately.

SORBET RECIPES

FRESH FRUIT BANANA SORBET

Prep: 10 minutes.   Freeze Time: 24 hours.   Serves: 6

- 6 ripe bananas (approximately), peeled, cut into 1/2-inch slices (4 cups banana)

UTENSILS

- Spoon

Instructions

1. Fill an empty CREAMi Deluxe Pint to MAX FILL line with the recommended fresh fruit.
2. With the back of a heavy kitchen utensil, such as a ladle or potato masher, then firmly press the fruit below the MAX FILL line, compacting it into a homogeneous mixture to create space for more fruit.
3. Continue to add more fruit and pressing down with a heavy utensil until all fruit is pressed into the Deluxe Pint just below the MAX FILL line. Place the storage lid on the Deluxe Pint and for 24 hrs freeze it.
4. Place the pint in the outer bowl, install the Creamerizer Paddle onto the outer bowl lid, and then lock the lid assembly on the outer bowl. Position the bowl assembly on the motor base and twist the handle right to lift the platform and lock it in place.
5. Select TOP, FULL, or BOTTOM and use the dial to choose SORBET.
6. Remove the sorbet from the Deluxe Pint after processing is complete, and serve immediately.

BOOZY PASSION PEACH SORBET

Prep: 5 minutes.   Total Time: 24 hours 5 minutes.   Serving: 4

- 1 1/2 cups TRULY Passionfruit Seltzer
- 4 tablespoons + 1 1/2 teaspoons raw agave nectar
- 1 1/2 cans (15 1/4 ounces) peaches in heavy syrup, drained, syrup discarded

UTENSILS

- Large Bowl
- Whisk

Instructions

1. whisk the seltzer in a large bowl and agave together until the agave is dissolved.
2. Pour peaches into an empty CREAMi Pint up to the MAX FILL line. Pour the seltzer and agave mixture over the peaches up to the MAX FILL line. Cover with the storage lid and for 24 hours freeze it.
3. Remove the Deluxe Pint from the freezer and the lid from the Deluxe Pint. Add the pour-in into the MAX FILL line. Place the pint in the outer bowl, install the Creamerizer Paddle onto the outer bowl lid, and then lock the lid assembly on the outer bowl. Position the bowl assembly on the motor base and twist the handle right to lift the platform and lock it in place.
4. Select TOP, FULL, or BOTTOM then also use the dial to choose SORBET.
5. Remove the sorbet from the pint once processing is complete and then serve immediately.

CONCORD GRAPE SORBET

Prep :7 minutes.   **Total Time: 24 hours 7 minutes.**
Servings: 4

- 1 cup + 2 tablespoons frozen concentrate of grape juice / 270g frozen grape juice concentrate
- 2 1/4 cups water / 533g water
- 1 1/2 tablespoons lemon juice

UTENSILS

- Medium Bowl
- Whisk

Instructions

1. In a medium-sized bowl, combine all ingredients and whisk until well blended.
2. Fill up the mixture into an empty CREAMi Deluxe Pint. Cover with the storage lid and for 24 hours freeze it.
3. Remove the Deluxe Pint from the freezer and the lid from the Deluxe Pint. Add the pour-in into the MAX FILL line. Place the pint in the outer bowl, install the Creamerizer Paddle onto the outer bowl lid, and then lock the lid assembly on the outer bowl. Position the bowl assembly on the motor base and twist the handle right to lift the platform and lock it in place.
4. Choose TOP, FULL, or BOTTOM and then use the dial to select SORBET.
5. Take out the sorbet from the pint once the process is completed and then serve immediately.

EASY PINEAPPLE SORBET

Prep : 1 minute.   **Total Time: 24 hours 1 minute.**
Servings: 4

- 2 cans (20 ounces each) Dole Pineapple Chunks, drained, with reserved liquid

Instructions

1. Fill an empty CREAMi Deluxe Pint with 3 cups of fruit chunks up to the MAX FILL line. Then, cover the fruit with 1 cup of liquid from the can up to the MAX FILL line. For a smaller portion, use a smaller can and fill below the MAX FILL line. Seal the pint with the storage lid and for 24 hrs freeze it.
2. Take the Deluxe Pint out of the freezer and then remove the lid. Refer to the quick start guide for bowl assembly and also unit interaction information.
3. Choose TOP, FULL, or BOTTOM and then use the dial to select SORBET.
4. Remove the sorbet once the process is completed and then serve immediately.

BOOZY STRAWBERRY SORBET

Prep : 5 minutes.   Total Time: 24 hours 5 minutes
Serving Size: 4

- 4 1/2 cups fresh strawberries, stems removed
- 1/2 cup water / 120g water
- 1/2 cup granulated sugar / 100g granulated sugar
- 1 cup + 2 tablespoons TRULY Berry Punch / 150g TRULY Berry Punch

UTENSILS

- Blender
- Fine-Mesh Strainer

Instructions

1. In a blender, combine all ingredients and blend on high for 1 min or until smooth.
2. Strain the base through a fine-mesh strainer to remove seeds and pour into an empty CREAMi Deluxe Pint. Cover with the storage lid and for 24 hrs freeze it.
3. Remove the Deluxe Pint from the freezer and the lid from the Deluxe Pint. Add the pour-in into the MAX FILL line. Place the pint in the outer bowl, install the Creamerizer Paddle onto the outer bowl lid, and then lock the lid assembly on the outer bowl. Position the bowl assembly on the motor base and twist the handle right to lift the platform and lock it in place.
4. Choose TOP, FULL, or BOTTOM, then also use the dial to select SORBET.
5. Remove the sorbet from the pint once processing is complete and then serve immediately.

FROZEN DRINK RECIPES

PALOMA

Prep: 3 minutes. Freeze Time: 24 hours. Serves: 2

Freezing Ingredients:
- 1 1/2 cups grapefruit juice / 345g grapefruit juice
- 1/3 cup simple syrup / 77g simple syrup
- 1/4 cup + 2 tablespoons lime juice / 87g lime juice
- Pinch of salt

For Processing:
- Pour-in: equal parts tequila and orange juice

UTENSILS
- Spoon

Instructions

1. In the Deluxe Pint up to the DRINKABLE FILL line, pour the grapefruit juice, simple syrup, lime juice, and salt.
2. Stir to combine the mixture and then place the storage lid on the Deluxe Pint and for 24 hours freeze it.
3. Remove the Deluxe Pint from the freezer and take off the lid. Add pour-in to the MAX FILL line. Place the pint in the outer bowl, install the Creamerizer Paddle onto the outer bowl lid, and then lock the lid assembly on the outer bowl. Position the bowl assembly on the motor base and twist the handle right to lift the platform and lock it in place. Select FULL, and use the dial to select FROZEN DRINK.
4. Transfer the frozen Paloma to a glass when processing is complete and serve immediately.

MAI TAI

Prep 3 mins.   Freeze Time 24 hours.   Serves 2

Ingredients for Freezing:
- 1/4 cup Torani Orange Syrup / 60g Torani Orange Syrup
- 1/2 cup lime juice / 115g lime juice
- 1/2 cup pineapple nectar / 115g pineapple nectar
- 1/4 teaspoon almond extract
- 1 cup water / 236g water

Ingredients for Processing (Pour-in):
- 1/2 cup dark rum
- 1/4 cup Triple sec

UTENSILS
- Spoon

Instructions

1. Combine orange syrup, lime juice, pineapple nectar, almond extract, and water in an empty CREAMi Deluxe Pint.
2. Stir well and freeze with the storage lid for 24 hours.
3. Remove the Deluxe Pint from the freezer and the lid from the Deluxe Pint. Add the pour-in into the MAX FILL line. Place the pint in the outer bowl, install the Creamerizer Paddle onto the outer bowl lid, and then lock the lid assembly on the outer bowl. Position the bowl assembly on the motor base and twist the handle right to lift the platform and lock it in place.
4. Select FULL, then choose the FROZEN DRINK setting.
5. Once processed, transfer the Margarita to a glass and then serve immediately.

MANGO MARGARITA

Preparation: 3 minutes. Freeze Time: 24 hours. Serves: 1

For Freezing:
- 1/2 cup Torani Mangonada Syrup / 170g Torani Mangonada Syrup
- 1/4 cup lime juice / 58g lime juice
- 1/4 cup mango nectar / 60g mango nectar
- 1 cup water / 236g water

For Processing:
- Pour-in: 1/2 cup tequila,
  1/4 cup lime juice

UTENSILS

- Spoon

Instructions

1. Pour the mangonada syrup, mango nectar, 1/4 cup lime juice, water to an empty CREAMi Deluxe Pint.
2. Stir to combine the mixture, place the storage lid on the pint and for 24 hours freeze it.
3. Remove the Deluxe Pint from the freezer and the lid from the Deluxe Pint. Add the pour-in into the MAX FILL line. Place the pint in the outer bowl, install the Creamerizer Paddle onto the outer bowl lid, and then lock the lid assembly on the outer bowl. Position the bowl assembly on the motor base and twist the handle right to lift the platform and lock it in place.
4. Select your processing zone FULL, then after use the dial to select FROZEN DRINK.
5. Transfer the margarita to a glass when the process is complete and serve immediately.

MANGO LASSI

Preparation: 3 minutes.   Freeze Time: 24 hours.   Serves: 1

For Freezing:
- 2 cups mango juice or mango puree /500g mango juice or mango puree
- 1/4 cup cashew yogurt / 61g cashew yogurt
- 1 tablespoon agave

For Processing:
- Pour-in: oat milk

UTENSILS
- Spoon

Instructions

1. Put the mango juice or puree, cashew yogurt and agave into an empty CREAMi Deluxe Pint.
2. Stir to combine the mixture, place the storage lid on the Deluxe Pint and for 24 hours freeze it.
3. Remove the Deluxe Pint from the freezer and the lid from the Deluxe Pint. Add the pour-in into the MAX FILL line. Place the pint in the outer bowl, install the Creamerizer Paddle onto the outer bowl lid, and then lock the lid assembly on the outer bowl. Position the bowl assembly on the motor base and twist the handle right to lift the platform and lock it in place.
4. Select FULL, and use the dial to select FROZEN DRINK.
5. Transfer the drink to a glass once processing is complete and serve immediately.

FROZEN GRASSHOPPER

Prep: 8 minutes.   Freeze Time: 24 hours.   Servings: 2

Ingredients for Freezing:
- 2 1/4 cups half & half / 540g half & half
- 5 leaves fresh mint, minced
- 1/2 teaspoon mint extract
- 1-2 drops green food color

Ingredients for Processing:
- Pour-in: Equal parts crème de cacao and crème de menthe

UTENSILS
- Spoon

Instructions

1. Place the half & half, minced fresh mint, mint extract, and green food color into an empty CREAMi Deluxe Pint up to the DRINKABLE FILL line.
2. Stir the mixture to combine. Put the storage lid on the Deluxe Pint and for 24 hours freeze it.
3. Remove the Deluxe Pint from the freezer and the lid from the Deluxe Pint. Add the pour-in into the MAX FILL line. Place the pint in the outer bowl, install the Creamerizer Paddle onto the outer bowl lid, and then lock the lid assembly on the outer bowl. Position the bowl assembly on the motor base and twist the handle right to lift the platform and lock it in place.
4. Select FULL, then use the dial to select FROZEN DRINK.
5. Transfer the frozen grasshopper shake to a glass once the processing is complete and then serve immediately.

FROZEN GRAPEFRUIT CRUSH

Prep: 4 minutes.   Freeze Time: 24 hours.   Servings: 2

Ingredients for Freezing:
- 1 3/4 cups grapefruit juice / 415g grapefruit juice
- 1/2 cup simple syrup / 113g simple syrup
- 2 tablespoons lime juice

Ingredients for Processing (Pour-in):
- - Equal parts 1/2 vodka and 1/2 triple sec

UTENSILS
- Spoon

Instructions

1. Place the grapefruit juice, lime juice and simple syrup in an empty CREAMi Deluxe Pint up unto the DRINKABLE FILL line.
2. Stir the mixture to combine. Cover the Deluxe Pint with the storage lid and for 24 hours freeze it.
3. Remove the Deluxe Pint from the freezer and the lid from the Deluxe Pint. Add the pour-in into the MAX FILL line. Place the pint in the outer bowl, install the Creamerizer Paddle onto the outer bowl lid, and then lock the lid assembly on the outer bowl. Position the bowl assembly on the motor base and twist the handle right to lift the platform and lock it in place.
4. Select FULL, then use the dial to select FROZEN DRINK.
5. Transfer the grapefruit crush to a glass once the processing is complete and then serve immediately.

HURRICANE

Prep 3 mins.   Freeze Time 24 hours.   Serves 2

Ingredients for Freezing:
- 3/4 cup Torani Passionfruit Syrup / 180g Torani Passionfruit Syrup
- 1/2 cup orange juice / 120g orange juice
- 1/4 cup lime juice / 60g lime juice
- 2 tablespoons grenadine

Ingredients for Processing:
- - Equal parts white rum and dark rum

UTENSILS
- Spoon

Instructions

1. Combine passion fruit syrup, orange juice, lime juice, and grenadine in an empty CREAMi Deluxe Pint.
2. Stir well and freeze with the storage lid for 24 hours.
3. Remove the Deluxe Pint from the freezer and the lid from the Deluxe Pint. Add the pour-in into the MAX FILL line. Place the pint in the outer bowl, install the Creamerizer Paddle onto the outer bowl lid, and then lock the lid assembly on the outer bowl. Position the bowl assembly on the motor base and twist the handle right to lift the platform and lock it in place.
4. Select FULL, then use the dial to select FROZEN DRINK.
5. Transfer the Hurricane to a glass once processed and then serve immediately.

FROZEN PAIN KILLER

Prep: 8 minutes.   Freeze Time: 24 hours.   Servings: 2

Ingredients for Freezing:
- 1 cup pineapple juice / 236g pineapple juice
- 1/2 cup orange juice / 113g orange juice
- 3/4 cup coconut cream / 177g coconut cream
- 1/4 teaspoon nutmeg

Ingredients for Processing (Pour-in):
- - Equal parts 1/2 dark rum and
- 1/2 orange juice

UTENSILS
- Spoon

Instructions

1. Pour pineapple juice, orange juice, coconut cream, and nutmeg in an empty CREAMi Deluxe Pint up to the DRINKABLE FILL line.
2. Stir the mixture to combine. Place the storage lid on the Deluxe Pint and for 24 hrs freeze it.
3. Remove the Deluxe Pint from the freezer and the lid from the Deluxe Pint. Add the pour-in into the MAX FILL line. Place the pint in the outer bowl, install the Creamerizer Paddle onto the outer bowl lid, and then lock the lid assembly on the outer bowl. Position the bowl assembly on the motor base and twist the handle right to lift the platform and lock it in place.
4. Select FULL, then use the dial to select FROZEN DRINK.
5. Transfer the pain killer to a glass once the processing is complete and then serve immediately.

FROZEN LIMONCELLO

Prep: 3 mins.   Freeze Time: 24 hours.   Serves: 2

Ingredients for Freezing:
- 113g raw agave nectar / 1/2 cup raw agave nectar
- 230g (1 cup) premade lemonade
- 3/4 cup water / 170g water

Ingredients for Processing (Pour-in):
- Equal parts limoncello and water

UTENSILS
- Spoon

Instructions

1. Pour the agave nectar, lemonade, and water into an empty CREAMi Deluxe Pint up to the DRINKABLE FILL line.
2. Stir the mixture until combined. Place the storage lid on the Deluxe Pint and for 24 hrs freeze it.
3. Remove the Deluxe Pint from the freezer and the lid from the Deluxe Pint. Add the pour-in into the MAX FILL line. Place the pint in the outer bowl, install the Creamerizer Paddle onto the outer bowl lid, and then lock the lid assembly on the outer bowl. Position the bowl assembly on the motor base and twist the handle right to lift the platform and lock it in place.
4. Select FULL, then use the dial to select FROZEN DRINK.
5. Transfer the Limoncello to a glass once the processing is complete and then serve immediately.

FROZEN KYIV MULE

Prep: 3 mins.   Freeze Time: 24 hours.   Serves: 2

Ingredients for Freezing:
- 1 1/2 cups water / 360g water
- 57g lime juice / 1/4 cup lime juice
- 3 tablespoons ginger juice
- 1/4 cup + 2 tablespoons mint syrup / 85g mint syrup

Ingredients for Processing (Pour-in):
- Equal parts ginger beer and Ukrainian vodka

UTENSILS
- Spoon

Instructions

1. Pour the water, ginger juice, lime juice and syrup in an empty CREAMi Deluxe Pint up unto the DRINKABLE FILL line.
2. Stir the mixture until combined. Place the storage lid on the Deluxe Pint and for 24 hrs freeze it.
3. Remove the Deluxe Pint from the freezer and the lid from the Deluxe Pint. Add the pour-in into the MAX FILL line. Place the pint in the outer bowl, install the Creamerizer Paddle onto the outer bowl lid, and then lock the lid assembly on the outer bowl. Position the bowl assembly on the motor base and twist the handle right to lift the platform and lock it in place.
4. Select FULL, then use the dial to select FROZEN DRINK.
5. Transfer the frozen Kyiv mule to a glass once the processing is complete, garnish with fresh mint, and serve immediately.

FINAL THOUGHT AND ENCOURAGEMENT

First off, big high-fives to you for diving into the tasty world of homemade frozen treats. Whether you've already made a bunch or you're just getting started, every time you scoop into your creation, it's like making a little memory in your kitchen. How cool is that?

Guess what? There are no rules when it comes to making your own frozen treats. Don't be afraid to mix things up, toss in your favorite candies, or even try out a funky flavor combo. This is your time to be a dessert inventor, so let your ideas flow and see what kind of delicious magic you can whip up.

Here's a secret ingredient to making your treats even better – sharing them! Imagine surprising your family with a batch of your own ice cream or having a fun ice cream party with your pals. It's like spreading joy and sweetness all around – a win-win!

Hey, if things don't turn out exactly like you planned on your first try, no big deal. Making awesome frozen treats is a learning adventure. Each time you mix, freeze, and taste, you're getting better and having fun. So keep at it, and soon you'll be a dessert-making expert!

So, my sweet friends, as you continue your frozen treat adventure with your trusty Ninja Creami Deluxe, remember to have a blast, try new things, and savor every tasty moment. Your kitchen is now a dessert wonderland waiting for your next sweet creation. Go on, make some sweet memories, and let the dessert party continue!

CONVERSION MEASUREMENT

Volume Measurements:
1 teaspoon (tsp) = 5 milliliters (ml)
1 tablespoon (tbsp) = 15 milliliters (ml)
1 fluid ounce (fl oz) = 30 milliliters (ml)
1 cup (c) = 240 milliliters (ml)
1 pint (pt) = 480 milliliters (ml)
1 quart (qt) = 960 milliliters (ml)
1 gallon (gal) = 3.8 liters (L)

Weight Measurements:
1 ounce (oz) = 28 grams (g)
1 pound (lb) = 16 ounces (oz)=
$$454 \text{ grams (g)}$$

Common Ingredient Conversions:
1 stick of butter = 1/2 cup = 113 grams
1 c of all-purpose flour = 120 grams
1 c of granulated sugar = 200 grams
1 c of powdered sugar = 120 grams
1 c of brown sugar = 220 grams
1 cup of milk = 240 milliliters
1 cup of heavy cream = 240 milliliters
1 cup of yogurt = 240 grams

TROUBLESHOOTING COMMON ISSUES

Issue #1: My Frozen Treat is Too Soft

If your ice cream, sorbet, or frozen yogurt is turning out too soft and not holding its shape, there could be a couple of reasons why. First, make sure that you've followed the recipe instructions carefully and that your ingredients are properly chilled before churning. Additionally, try freezing your mixture for a bit longer before churning to help it set up properly.

Issue #2: My Frozen Treat is Too Hard

On the flip side, if your frozen treat is coming out too hard and difficult to scoop, you might need to adjust your recipe or churning time. Try using less sugar or adding a bit more liquid to your mixture to help keep it softer. You can also try reducing the churning time to prevent over-freezing.

Issue #3: My Frozen Treat Has Ice Crystals

Nobody likes icy, grainy ice cream! If you're noticing ice crystals in your frozen treats, it could be due to a couple of factors. Make sure that your mixture is properly chilled before churning and avoid over-churning, as this can introduce too much air into the mixture and cause it to freeze unevenly. Storing your frozen treats in an airtight container in the coldest part of your freezer can also help prevent ice crystal formation.

Issue #4: My Ninja Creami Deluxe is Making Strange Noises

If you're hearing unusual noises coming from your Ninja Creami Deluxe while it's in operation, it could be a sign of a mechanical issue. Check to make sure that all the parts are properly assembled and that there are no obstructions blocking the paddle or motor.

Issue #5: My Frozen Treat Tastes Funny

Finally, if your frozen treat is coming out with a strange taste or odor, it could be due to a couple of factors. First, make sure that all your ingredients are fresh and haven't expired. Additionally, be mindful of any strong-smelling foods that you're adding to your mixture, as they can sometimes overpower the flavor of your frozen treat.

Printed in Great Britain
by Amazon